BALLISTIC BEGINNINGS

Andy Robb

Ballistic Beginnings

Copyright © 2001 John Hunt Publishing Ltd
46a West Street, Alresford, Hants SO24 9AU, UK

Published in 2003 in the United States of America by Abingdon Press,
201 Eighth Avenue South, Nashville, TN 37203

Text © 2001 Andy Robb
Illustrations © 2001 Andy Robb

ISBN 0-687-02336-X

Design by Nautilus Design, UK

Scriptures quoted from the Good News Bible published by The Bible
Societies/HarperCollins Publishers Ltd., UK,
© American Bible Society,1966, 1971, 1976, 1992

Printed by Tien Wah Press Ltd, Singapore

CONTENTS

Introduction

What's the most boring thing you can think of? Okay, now multiply it by a zillion.

That's how boring a lot of people think the Bible is. The funny thing is, most people who think the Bible is mega mind-numbingly boring have never even read it! Crazy or what?!

Imagine turning down a triple whopper chicken, cheese and yogurt burger with gherkin and custard relish just because you'd never tried it...

On second thought that wasn't such a good suggestion. But you get my point?

I mean, I'll bet you didn't even know that the Bible's got advertisements in it to tell people what's going to happen in the future or that it told people that the world was round thousands of years before we'd worked it out.

There's so much stuff in the Bible we won't be able to look at every bit of it but the bits we've chosen will hopefully make you start to realize that the Bible maybe isn't quite so boring as you thought.

Have fun!

So What's The Bible All About?

The Bible isn't just one whopping great book.

It's actually 66 not-quite-so-whopping books all whacked together like a sort of mini library.

The first book in the Bible is called Genesis, which was also the name of a pop group your parents once liked but they won't admit to it even if you hang them from the ceiling by their toenails... and the last book is called Revelation which as far as I know it wasn't the name of a pop group your parents once liked.

To keep things simple, the Bible is mainly about two things.

God.
And people.

Who wrote the Bible?
People.

Who decided what to write about?
God.

So how did they know what God wanted them to write?
Did God send an e-mail?

Not quite.
Here's one way of looking at it.
Imagine two people in love.

Enough of that!
Sorry, have I put you off your lunch?
When people are in love with each other all they want to do is
spend every waking hour gazing lovingly into each other's eyes.
(I know, it's horrible, isn't it!)

The way they hug and cuddle each other you wonder whether they've been permanently glued to each other for all eternity.

It even gets to the point where they start to think each other's thoughts.

Well, that's sort of what it was like for the guys who wrote the Bible (without the cuddling bit).

I THINK HIS EXCUSE THAT HE OVERSLEEPS SO THAT GOD CAN SPEAK TO HIM IN DREAMS IS WEARING A BIT THIN!

They spent so much time with God that they got to know what God was thinking and what he wanted to say.

It was as if God had written it.

So what sort of things does God want to say to us?

For starters, the Bible tells us that there is a God and that God made you and me and the whole universe.

It also tells us that God wants us to be God's friends and how we can do that.

What good is a book that was written *even before* my mom and dad were born? People might not wear silly costumes like they did in the past but God hasn't changed a bit so what God had to say to people with funny headdresses and sandals thousands of years ago is still important for us.

This Holy Happenings book is all about how everything began and it's all taken out of just one book in the Bible...yes, you guessed it, it's **GENESIS**.

(By the way, I was only joking about hanging your parents upside down by their toenails - nose hairs work much better!!!)

How It All Began

You've probably heard lots of different ideas about how the world, the universe and everything started.

HEY, WHERE DID I SUDDENLY COME FROM?

Most of the incredible ideas people come up with don't even include God which, to be perfectly honest, is a little bit odd. Here's a question.

Can you think of anything you own, like CDs, clothes, computers, deodorant sprays (no, I'm not saying you smell, honest) that hasn't been made by someone?

No, nor can I?

Everything needs *someone* to design it and make it. It's the same with the planets and animals and trees. To imagine that your sneakers just sort of gradually happened from nothing is just about as mind-bogglingly bizarre as believing that your pet cat (or goldfish or whatever) simply came from nowhere.

So, the Bible not only tells us *how* it all happened but also *who* it was who made it happen.
Neat, huh?
Now, here's the good bit.
When God made everything God didn't do it like we'd do with a lump of modeling clay and make a nice little bumpy mountain here and a big, fat wibbly wobbly hippopotamus there.

What God did was altogether unusual to say the least.
Have you ever seen soldiers being ordered around by their
commanding officer?
They obediently do exactly as he tells them.
Well, that's what it was like when God created the universe.
God simply commanded it to happen with God's voice...and it
did.
Let's take a look at God's creation timetable.

Day One

One of the hardest questions to answer is 'who made God?'.
It's hard to answer because nobody did!
The Bible says that God's *always* been around.
That's hard to imagine isn't it because everything has a begin-
ning and an end.
But God isn't like us.
You and I have birthdays so we know exactly how old we are
and what period of the world's history we live in.
The Bible says that God is *outside* of time.
Take a look at this line.

It has a beginning and it has an end.
Just like us.
Now let's draw a circle round the line.

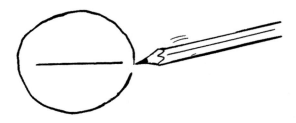

That's where God's at - *outside* of time.
When God made the universe and everything God was also making time at the same time, if you see what I mean.
Clever, eh?

First time didn't exist and then, bingo, it did.

And *that's* how the first bit of the Bible kicks off.

To be honest, you wouldn't have wanted to take a holiday on planet earth at this particular moment not unless you liked things dark and nothingy.

Formless and desolate is how the Bible puts it.

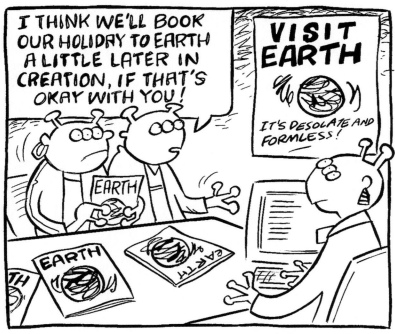

Actually the earth was also rather on the wet side due in the most part to it being not much more than a big ball of water.

Just when you were beginning to think that's all there was to it, God commanded light to appear.

God called the light 'Day' and the darkness 'Night' and that was
the end of Day One and if I say it myself a rather impressive
day's work.

Day Two

When the year 2000 came around, people from all across the
world did all sorts of spectacular things to celebrate it.
In London they constructed a gigantic dome-shaped building to
house a millennium exhibition.

What nobody realized was that it had all been done
before...and much, much bigger.
On the second day of God's creation the Bible tells us that God
decided to do something about the soggy wetness of the earth.
Like I said, it was still little more than one big swirling ocean
and not much good for anything else unless you were really into
swimming or deep sea diving.
So, God made a dome.
A big dome at that.
Big enough to cover the whole earth and separate the water
into two places.
The water above the dome God called 'Sky'.
Now, you're probably wondering what possible use God could
have for keeping a rather large supply of wetness hanging over
the earth.

The answer is simple.

It was probably stored in the form of water vapor and gave the earth a nice protective layer.

It would also keep the earth warm, a bit like a greenhouse.

A good God idea if ever I saw one.

Day Three

The next thing God did was to collect all the water together in one place so that there was dry land, which meant that at long last the seaside had been invented, not that there was anyone around to enjoy it yet.

God called the land 'Earth' and the water, yes, you guessed it, 'Sea'.

Now, here comes the good bit.

The plants.

The good thing about being God is that when you need to do a spot of planting you don't have to pop down to the garden center to have a look round...you just create whatever it is you want.

Being God you don't even need to bother with planting fiddly seeds.
One minute there wasn't anything remotely plant-like anywhere, then, the next minute the earth was completely covered with trees and plants and flowers and fruit and crops and, well, every sort of plant that ever there was.

And the good part of it all was that everything had seeds in it to keep them reproducing over and over again.
It was *so* amazingly brilliant that the Bible even tells us that God was pleased with it.

And so God should be.

Just think, every plant or tree or flower you see around you can be traced back to that one moment in creation.

Awesome!

Day Four

If you know anything about plants you'll know they need a good dose of sunlight to keep them alive.

Using sunlight, plants also produce oxygen for us to breathe which is why God made the sun next.

God put the sun just the right distance from the Earth (93 million miles if you must know). A little bit closer and we'd all be burned to a frazzle.

A little further away and we'd all be frozen like a pack of fish sticks.

And then there's the moon.

Some people can't go to sleep without a bedside light on.
They don't need *much* light, just a bit of a glow will do fine.
That's precisely what the moon is.

The moon reflects the sun's light and gives us a softer light to see by at night.
Isn't God thoughtful.
Like the sun, the moon is also just the right distance away from the Earth.
The moon's gravity tugs at our oceans and causes the twice-daily tides which is God's ingenious way of keeping our harbors and river mouths clean.
If the moon were a bit larger or a bit closer it would cause huge

tidal waves to sweep over our shores twice a day making life impossible in many parts of the world.

The way *God's* done it, it's just perfect.
To put the finishing touches to a busy day, God set the stars in the sky.

Did you know that there are *billions* of stars up there which form millions and millions of galaxies?
It makes you wonder whether God put them up there just to show us how amazing and big God is.

Fascinating Fact:

An eclipse of the sun (that's when the moon goes in front of the sun), can only happen because of the incredible precision with which these two planets have been placed in space. The moon has a diameter of 2000 miles and fits exactly over the sun (from our viewpoint) which is exactly 800,000 miles across. Also the sun is exactly 400 times further away from us than the moon. Staggering or what?!

Day Five

What came first, the chicken or the egg? That's what the old riddle asks.

Well, the good news is that the Bible gives you the answer and it's definitely *not* the egg.

Today in God's diary it's 'Making Birds And Fishes Day'.
No waiting around for eggs to hatch, just instant birds flying
through the sky.
And even the fish didn't need swimming lessons.
They just took to it like a fish to water.

Fascinating Fact:

*People copied the design of birds to build airplanes
but birds are still much better fliers because their feathers
can bend. They also have several different types
of feathers on their wings. Some pull them through the
air while others give them the lift they need. The tail
feathers are there to steer and balance the bird. Birds
even use special feathers on their wing tips to take off
and land - just like the flaps on an airplane's wings.
But God thought of it first.*

Day Six

Phew! What a busy week it's been.

Anyway, it's quiz time.

Think of a land-based animal beginning with each letter of the alphabet and write your answers down below.

(Ask a grown-up if you're really stuck. They love coming up with clever answers!)

A

B

C

D

E

F

G

H
I
J
K
L
M
N
O
P
Q
R
S
T
U
V
W
X
Y
Z

Finished?

(You might have been able to complete it with just the odd 'X' - ception!)

On Day Six of Creation the Bible says that God made every animal that ever there was. That's thousands and thousands of different kinds.

Not only that but God made them so that they could have babies of their very own so that they could fill the earth.

Aah!

Pity your sneakers couldn't do that then you'd never have to buy another pair.

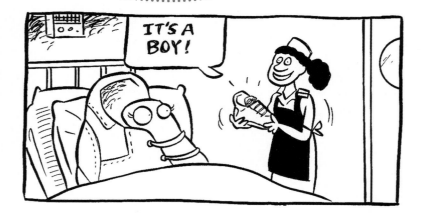

Now let me think, there was one thing more that God made on Day Six.
Now, what was it?
Ah, yes.!
People.
That was it.

"Why didn't God make people when God made the rest of the animals?" you may ask.
And that's a very good question.
The answer is very simple.
People weren't going to be like all the other creatures God had made.
People were going to be made in God's *likeness*.

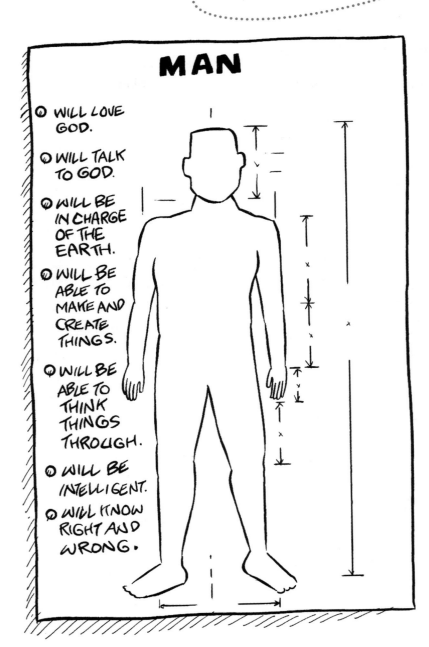

These were all things none of the other creatures were able to do.

One more thing.

The way that God chose to make his first person was altogether different from how God created everything else.

CREATION COOKERY COURSE
HOW TO MAKE A MAN
(IN ONE EASY-ISH LESSON)

1. Take one handful of soil from the ground.

2. Mold skilfully into the shape of a man (Avoid using a gingerbread man cutter - far too naff!)

3. When completely satisfied with result, breathe gently up the man's nostrils until he springs to life.

* FOR BEST RESULTS, USE MAN ON DAY OF MAKING!

God decided to call the man 'Adam' which coincidentally *means* 'man' which is quite handy.

One more day to go.

Here's some things that *God* made and some things that *people* have made by copying God's designs.

Draw a line to link God's original design with the man-made copies.

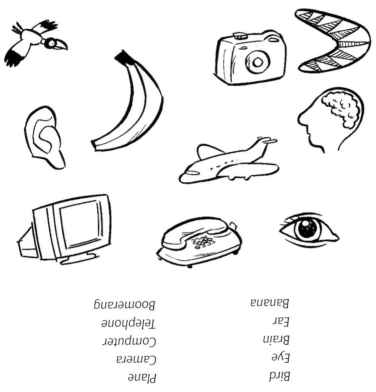

Boomerang   Banana
Telephone   Ear
Computer   Brain
Camera   Eye
Plane   Bird

Only kidding with the last one - just my idea of a little joke -
A very little joke - the Editor!

Day Seven

What do you mean, there's nothing on it. Of *course* there's nothing on it.

It's *blank* because God did *nothing* on the seventh day of Creation.

God simply rested because there wasn't any more creating to be done.

In fact God made the seventh day of the week a *special* day from then on for people to rest and worship God.

God always knows what's best for God's creation.

Holy Happenings Interesting Thought: Everyone round the world has a seven-day week. But why? It wouldn't have anything to do with God's first seven-day week, would it?

Round And Round The Garden

Most people have somewhere to live and many of us have gardens.

Adam was no exception.

He had a garden but not one with a fence round it and a shed at the bottom.

The garden that God made for Adam to live in was unlike any other garden you've ever seen.

God specially planted the garden for Adam in a place called Eden.

Nobody's *exactly* sure where it was but the Bible gives us a few clues which puts it somewhere around here...

What do you think was the first job anybody ever did in the history of the world?
Go on, have a guess!
Was it...

Mighty hunter? ☐

King? ☐

Super hero? ☐

Conqueror? ☐

Wrong!
It was...gardener.
Yep! God put Adam in charge of the **garden**.
Admittedly it was a garden you've not seen the like of before but, nevertheless, gardener was his job and gardening's what Adam did.
We got our artist to draw a picture of what *he* thought the Garden of Eden might have looked like.
Here it is...**with a few additional comments from the Editor!**

On second thought, I think we'll forget about that idea!

An Inside Job!

You know those crime films where a bank is robbed and you find out that it was the bank manager who was doing it all along?

Well, that's sort of what happened to our Adam. God not only gave him the job of cultivating the Garden of Eden but God also put him in charge of *guarding* it.

Slap bang in the middle of the garden stood two trees.
The tree that gives knowledge of what is good and what is bad.
And the tree that gives life.

Like a bank manager is in charge of the money in the bank and isn't expected to steal any of it, Adam was in charge of guarding the trees and under strict instructions not to eat anything whatsoever from the tree of the knowledge of good and

bad or he would be in *big* trouble.
Let's not beat about the bush, he'd be more than just in big trouble, he would **die**.

You'll have to wait a little bit longer to find out whether Adam did a good job leaving the trees alone or whether he was a naughty boy, but first Adam's got another very important job to do.

Name That Animal

You'd probably get the impression from *some* history books you read that the first people who lived on the earth weren't too bright and that they couldn't say much more than "UGH!".
(That's unless you speak a language where the word 'UGH' actually means something like 'Equilateral Triangle' or 'Cheese

and Tomatoes on Toast'.)

The Bible says that God put Adam in charge of giving *every* animal on the earth a name.
Just think how long *that* would take.

Adam wouldn't have got very far if the only word he'd known was 'Ugh!'.

Ask your mom and dad how long it took *them* to think of a
name for *you*.
I'll bet it took them a while.

As far as things like the skunks and other smelly animals were
concerned, if I were Adam, I'd probably just drop them a line
and tell them what I'd called them.
No need for a personal visit.
There are some aromas the Garden of Eden can well do without.

And then how on earth do you *remember* them all?

I'll Be Your Friend If You'll Be Mine

Because God was kind God realized that it wasn't going to be much fun for Adam being all alone.

Adam needed a friend but to be perfectly frank, it doesn't look like the animals are going to be much help at all.

Beddie-byes

There was nothing for it.

God needed to *make* a companion for Adam.

Since all the creating was finished God needed to make the companion out of something that was to hand, or more to the point, to *rib*.

God was going to whip out one of Adam's ribs and make him a wife.

As you can imagine, pulling out a rib isn't the nicest of operations, especially when it's *your* rib we're talking about, but God was one step ahead of the game and had put Adam into a nice deep sleep before he removed it.

Forceps.

Scalpel.

Anesthetic.

No, don't need any of *them*.

That's God for you.

Job done, God had made Adam his very own woman out of the rib.

Happy at last!

Would You Adam And Eve It?

(That's rhyming slang for 'Would you believe it?' if you really want to know - sorry, I'm just trying to be clever.)

Now, I'm afraid I've got a bit of bad news for you if you were expecting a happy ending. You'll have to read *Super Son* in the Holy Happenings series for one of those.

Sad to say, just when everything looked just perfect, God's enemy comes onto the scene.

Snakes Alive!

In Genesis, God's enemy is called a snake or serpent but his real name is Satan or sometimes the Devil.

Either way he was a nasty piece of work.

Sad to say he'd once been a top angel with God but had rebelled against God and was thrown out of heaven.

Satan now has only one main aim which is to destroy all the good things that God has made.

He wants *everyone* to rebel against God like he did.

Without warning, the Devil turns up in the Garden of Eden, and sets about spoiling things.

Let's be honest, Adam and his woman were pretty innocent (no, Adam hasn't quite got round to giving her a name yet, give him time).

Well they *must* have been innocent to be running round without any clothes on.

But hey, who's bothered?

If it doesn't embarrass you, then it doesn't embarrass me.

The Devil on the other hand was a cunning old fox (well snake, actually).
He started to sow seeds of doubt into the woman's innocent mind.

Let's EVE'S-drop on their conversation - **Not funny! - Editor.**

DID GOD **REALLY** TELL YOU NOT TO EAT FRUIT FROM ANY TREE IN THE GARDEN?

WE MAY EAT THE FRUIT OF ANY TREE IN THE GARDEN EXCEPT THE TREE IN THE MIDDLE OF IT. GOD TOLD US NOT TO EAT THE FRUIT FROM THAT TREE OR EVEN TOUCH IT! IF WE DO WE WILL DIE!

THAT'S NOT TRUE! GOD SAID THAT BECAUSE HE KNOWS THAT WHEN YOU EAT IT, YOU WILL BECOME LIKE HIM AND KNOW WHAT IS GOOD AND WHAT IS BAD!

The woman was enticed by the beauty of the tree and its wonderful fruit.
Then she thought how good it would be to be wise. Without another word she took some of the fruit and ate it.

Then she gave some of it to Adam, her husband and he also ate some.

At that moment their innocence was gone.

They suddenly realized that they were stark naked and had to make a couple of fig leaf cozzies in a hurry to cover themselves up. Okay, so maybe it's not the height of fashion but at least it does the job!

I'll bet the Devil was pleased with the way things had turned out. One thing's for certain... God wasn't.

EVE-ning Falls...And So Does ADAM!

When God turned up that evening they desperately tried to hide from God among the trees but without much luck.
Playing hide and seek with God is a bit of a joke when God can see *everything*!

Not only that, but Adam blamed the woman for getting him to eat the fruit then the woman blamed the snake.

Bet it's sometimes like that in your house when you're in trouble with your parents.

Fascinating Fact:

The Bible never mentions anything about an 'apple' in the story of Adam and Eve. All it says was that it was a fruit.

There was nothing for it but for God to punish **all three of them**.
Here's sort of how it went.

"Snake. You stand here today (well, you would do if you had legs), accused of a crime of the utmost slitheryness. By deception and cunning you did, on or around the beginning of creation, wilfully and wantonly trick this man and this woman into partaking of illegal food substances. Out of pure spite and jealousy you did all in your power to spoil things between God and these other two defendants."

"By the power vested in me by these courts, I hereby sentence you to crawl on your belly and eat dust for howsoever long you shall live."

"In view of the seriousness of your crime you will incur an additional punishment and it is this. From this time henceforth you and the woman and her offspring will be bitter enemies and one of them will, in due course, allowing for the passage of time, eventually destroy you."

"Bring on the next defendant."

"Woman. On or around the time of the beginning of creation, having been approached by that scurrilous reprobate, namely the snake, you did disobediently eat that which you had been expressly forbidden to even touch. It is not enough in a court of law to lay the blame at the feet of the snake, which you have tried unsuccessfully to do (not that he has feet, you understand, but you get my point). You stand here today accountable for your own actions, in the light of which it is my solemn and somber duty to pass sentence upon your crime against God."

"Woman, I sentence you to pain and trouble in childbirth. In the light of the fact that you have sinned against God (*Check out page 54 to find out all about 'sin'*) your husband will from this time and henceforth, rule over you."

"Call the last defendant."

"Adam. You stand here accused of flagrant rebellion and disobedience before God. Perhaps, with hindsight, you might have considered it somewhat unwise in the extreme to pay any attention whatsoever to the misinformed suggestions of your wife."

"Nevertheless, you did indeed listen to her and for what you have done the ground from which you presently gain your employment will be, from this moment onward, under a curse. The ground will now produce weeds and thorns and will no longer be pleasureable to tend. I sentence you to a lifetime of hard labor. In that you were formed by God from the soil of the earth, one day you will eventually die and return to that very same soil."

Fascinating Fact:

Only now did Adam give his wife a name, Eve, which here means 'life or living' because she was the mother of all people yet to come.

Although Adam and Eve were punished by God for their wrong-doing God didn't stop loving them or caring for them. The Bible tells us that, after all this, God even went to the trouble of making Adam and Eve proper clothes out of animal skins.

Because Adam and Eve had now been spoiled by sin, God couldn't allow them to live forever. (Yes, I know I said we were going to talk about what sin is, but you'll have to wait just a bit longer.)

Imagine a wormy apple overstaying its welcome.

Not a nice thought!

It's the same with *people* who have gone a bit rotten.

Adam and Eve could live forever if they ate fruit from the tree of life in the middle of the Garden of Eden.

But an earth full of sin-spoiled humans living for ever would not be a good move.

To prevent this, God took immediate action.

So, Adam and Eve were made to leave the Garden of Eden for good.
Adam and Eve lost their jobs as gardeners and cherubim guarded the garden with flaming swords that turned in all directions.
So that was that.
And to think it had all started out so nice.

Fascinating Fact:

Cherubim aren't fluffy pink flying babies that we often see in old paintings or on Valentine's Day cards. They were awesome and powerful winged creatures from heaven who served God.

The good bit is that although Adam and Eve broke their friendship with God, God was still in the business of trying to patch things up.
As you read through the other Boring Bible books, you'll see how hard God works to try and get people back to being God's friends.
And just in case you're wondering whether God's plan to bring people back into a friendship with God succeeds...it does!
But that's *another* story.

So, What Exactly Is Sin?

(I told you we'd eventually get round to it, didn't I?)

Sin is a word that the Bible uses a lot so we might as well get used to it.

To be honest, a lot of people would rather avoid the subject, but if you're up for it then so am I.

Here goes.

Sin is doing what God doesn't want us to do. (Or NOT doing what God DOES want us to do!)

That was easy wasn't it.

Well, that's probably the easiest part.

If we had the choice most of us would end up just doing the things we wanted to do, wouldn't we.

Because God made us, it's pretty obvious that God would be the best person to tell us what's good for us and what's bad for us.

Here's an example.

If you've got a Gameboy you're also going to get an instruction book.

The manufacturers haven't written it to *spoil* your enjoyment of the Gameboy, in fact, it's the complete opposite.

They want you to get the
absolute *best* out of it.
They don't want you pressing
the wrong button and
gumming up the thing.

All sin is, is people ignoring
God who made them and
doing what *they* want.
Doesn't sound like a good
idea to me.
Look where it landed Adam
and Eve!!!

God not only gave Adam the job of cultivating the Garden of
Eden but he put him in charge of it as well.

Adam's Family

(No, not *that* ADDAMS Family).

Adam and Eve were like no other people who've ever lived.

Each one of *us* starts out life in our mom's tum (or thereabouts) and nine months later out we pop, full of wind, sick and goodness knows what else to delight our parents with.

Over the years we grow and develop until we become fully grown humans.

That didn't happen for our first man and first lady.

They skipped the diapers, yukky baby foods, kindergarden, kids' TV, learning to ride a bike, being sent to bed early and heaps more.

They went straight from nothing to the full-size model with no stops in between.

One minute they *weren't* then, the next instant, kerzap!, there they were.

That must have been better than every theme park ride you've ever been on.

When Adam and Eve decided to have kids of their own they'd never even *seen* a baby before.

This was one human being that definitely *wasn't* going to start out full-size...thank goodness.

As it turned out it was a baby boy.

If soccer had been invented, Adam would have only been ten kids way from a full team, but unfortunately it hadn't so there was absolutely no point in calling the baby Maradonna or Pele. Instead they opted for 'Cain', which seemed to suit the lad.

The Bible doesn't say how long after but, in due course, the world's first family doubled its collection of babies with the birth of boy number two.
This one they called Abel.

Abel become a shepherd when he grew up.
And Cain became a farmer.
(I guess Adam and his kids must have liked the outdoor life - personally I'd have chosen something a little less rugged like a piano tuner or a teacher.)

Un-Happy Families

ABEL

ABEL
Offered the first lamb
from one of his sheep as
a sacrifice to God.
God was pleased - not so much
with what he gave but his attitude
of trust or faith in God.

CAIN

Cain was fuming with anger at having his offering rejected by God.

Or, more to the point, jealous that Abel had had *his* offering *accepted.*

Cain tricked Abel into going out into the countryside and then brutally murdered him in cold blood - his own brother - can you believe it?

The effects of sin were starting to take hold.
Cain was severely punished by God.
He was condemned to spend the rest of his days wandering the earth.

Fascinating Fact:

There is a well-known expression which goes:
"Am I my brother's keeper?"
That started its life in the Bible when God asked Cain
where Abel was and rather than admit he'd killed him
he gave this reply.

What Became Of Cain?

Cain's life wasn't *all* bad after that.
He got married.
Had a son, called Enoch.
Built a city.
His descendants even invented the harp and flute.
They also started using bronze and iron tools.

Fascinating Fact:

At this time in history people lived for a very long time which isn't quite so unbelievable as you may think. Don't forget that the earth was still covered with a water covering which not only protected people from harmful rays from the sun but also had other positive effects on their health to make them live longer and plants and animals grow larger.

Really old fossils that archaeologists have discovered show that in the past most things grew to a much, much bigger size. Only later on after the Flood, which we'll look at soon, did people's ages start to decrease.

By the time you get to Moses (you can find him in Holy Happenings book *Magnificent Moses*), God actually sets 120 years as the maximum age people can live to. Interestingly, however hard scientists try to make people live past this age, they can't!

So, let's see who were the longest livers back in those early days. (No, not like kidneys and livers - people who *lived* a long time type livers.)

The World's Oldest Men

Premier Division

1   Methuselah - lived 969 years. Died in the year of the Flood.
2   Jared - lived 962 years.
3   Noah - lived 950 years. It could have been only 600 if he hadn't been such a good man!
4   Adam - lived 930 years.
5   Seth - lived 912 years. He was Adam and Eve's third child.
6   Kenan - lived 910 years.
7   Enosh - lived 905 years. Around the time he was born people starting worshiping God.
8   Mahalalel - lived 895 years.

And then of course there's Enoch. Enoch was a bit unconventional to say the least. When Enoch was 365 years old (a mere youngster) God just took him away. He disappeared into thin air.
That's only because, as the Bible says, Enoch spent his life totally close to God so God didn't even allow him to suffer death.

From Bad To Worse

As the number of people on earth grew, so did their wickedness.
People had decided to live without God.
God was sorry he'd ever made them.
God made the decision to wipe his creation off the face of the earth, once and for all, with a flood.
It was going to be the biggest and most effective clean-up of the environment in the history of the world.
Hang on a minute.
Hold that water!
God's found one man who's not like the rest of them.

Meet Noah.
The Bible says that Noah had no faults, that he spent a lot of time with God and was the only good man of his time.

God spoke to Noah and told him God's plan.

God instructed Noah to build a boat big enough for himself, his family and some of every kind of animal that lived.

Actually, it wasn't going to be so much a boat as a box.

The biggest box the world had ever seen.

Another name for that sort of box is an ark.

The Bible tells us that Noah was a farmer so building a boat would have been a bit of a change.

Imagine having to build the world's biggest boat when maybe the biggest bit of woodwork you've done before is put up a couple of shelves.

God gave Noah detailed instructions of exactly how God wanted the ark to be built.

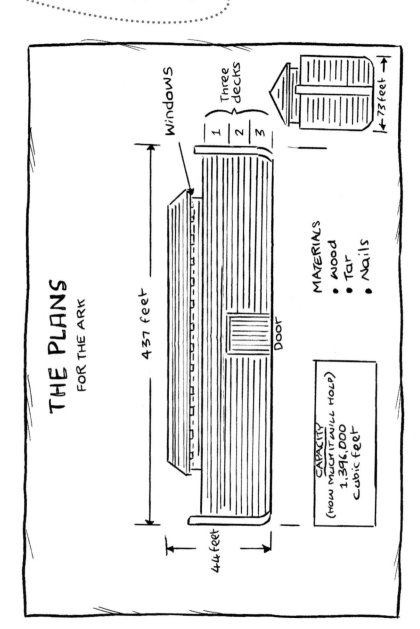

THE PLANS
FOR THE ARK

Windows

Three decks

1
2
3

73 feet

437 feet

Door

44 feet

MATERIALS
• Wood
• Tar
• Nails

CAPACITY
(HOW MUCH IT WILL HOLD)
1,396,000
cubic feet

Fascinating Fact:

Did you know that you could have fitted 432 double-decker buses into the ark - but buses weren't invented yet so Noah took animals instead!

The ark's length was six times longer than its width. Shipbuilders say that a boat built like this could tip over almost on to its side without capsizing.

Considering that the ark was built to *float* not to sail, it was the *safest* boat ever built.

The same word that the Bible uses to describe the ark is used later in the Bible to describe the watertight basket that saved Moses. Very interesting, eh?!

Which One Do You Think Is The Longest?

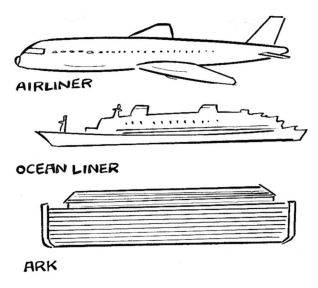

AIRLINER

OCEAN LINER

ARK

Answers: An airliner is about 220 feet long, an ocean liner is about 860 feet long and the ark was 437 feet long.

Meanwhile, Back In Noah's Neighborhood

Some Wild Guesses From The Holy Happening Wild Guess Department

Wild Guess Number One

As well as having his three sons, Shem, Ham and Japheth, to help build the ark, I wonder if Noah also employed the services of other people as well.

A boat that big (even though it could have taken up to 100 years to build) would have been a massive task in anyone's book. What do you think?

Wild Guess Number Two

Noah could well have been a very wealthy man.

Building a boat that size isn't cheap.

I wonder how much it would cost in today's money?

Wild Guess Number Three

Perhaps Noah even tried to persuade his neighbors to come on board, who knows.

Do you think he would?

Zoo Time

Not only did Noah have to *build* this whopper of a boat but God also gave him the job of gathering the animals to fill it.

The good news is that Noah didn't have to go out and capture them all himself.

The Bible says that God *sent* them to Noah.

These animals were going to repopulate the world after the terrible flood so there were two main requirements:

1 There needed to be a male and female of each species (pretty obvious really!)

2 They needed to be reasonably young so that they could mate.

This was good news for Noah fitting them all in.
Even the biggest creatures probably weren't anywhere near their full-grown size yet.
That's a relief!
What all those songs and rhymes about the ark *don't* tell you is that some of the animals didn't go into the ark two by two.
Some of them went in seven by *seven*.
So, why's that?
Did Noah have favorites?
Nothing of the sort.

As far as God was concerned there were two types of animals:
CLEAN and UNCLEAN.

The CLEAN animals could be burned as a sacrifice to please God as a sign of thanks to him, just like Abel did with his lamb, remember?
That's why more of them were needed.
They wouldn't *all* be used for breeding.
The UNCLEAN animals on the other hand were only in pairs because two was enough when all you needed them for was to mate.

Fascinating Fact:

Someone has cleverly calculated that the ark would have been capable of holding 125,280 sheep but that wouldn't be with room to breathe.
There are roughly 18,000 species of land animals.
Some would be larger than a sheep, some a lot smaller, but averaging that out there would have been room for two of each on just one of the ark's three decks leaving one deck for perhaps food and the third for Noah and his family.

Smell-O-Meter

Let's not beat about the bush.

An ark-full of animals must have been a bit on the stinky side to say the least.

Exactly how smelly you think it was is up to you.

Color in the Smell-O-Meter to show how smelly you reckon it was.

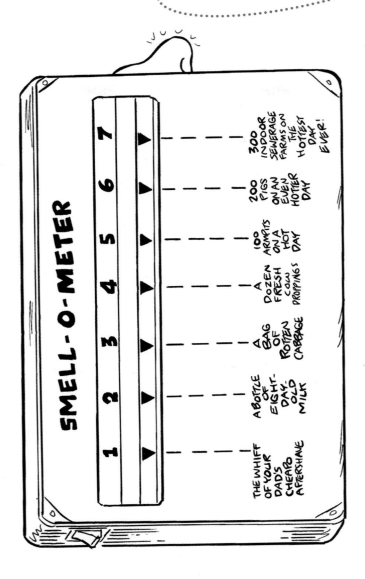

Flood Countdown

Just seven days to go and not a drop of rain in sight.

With one week to go God told Noah, his wife, his three sons
and their wives to enter the ark with all the animals.
Noah was now 600 years old, the ark had been 100 years in
the making and this was the very year that the world's oldest
man, Methuselah, had died aged 969.
It was as if God was saying that Methuselah's death signaled the
end of an era.

I wonder what Noah thought as he looked out from the ark
onto the neighboring towns and cities, knowing that by the end
of the week they would all be destroyed?
How Noah must have wanted to beg the people to change their
hearts toward God.
Perhaps God knew what Noah was thinking.
The door in the side of the ark could only be shut in *one* way
and by *one* person.
From the *outside* and by *God*.
God couldn't risk allowing even one single wicked person onto

that boat for fear of how they might ruin things once the flood had subsided.

One Week Later

With Noah, his family and all the animals safely on board there was just one job left for God to do.

The Bible tells us that on the seventeenth day of the second month, when Noah was 600 years old, God shut the door of the ark.

If anybody had had a last minute change of heart it was now too late.

It's like turning up at the port and finding that the departure gate is closed and you've missed your sailing.

But in this case there weren't going to be any more sailings.

There was only going to be one ark bobbing above the flood when it came.

And to be blunt, 100 years is more than enough time to get around to booking your ticket!

Weather News

Well, as we all know, the weather forecasters don't *always* get it right!

Sploosh!

After 100 years of waiting, the time had at last come.
Here comes the flood.
The thing is, it wasn't just one of those heavy downpour types of flood that you and I sometimes get.
You know the sort.
It rains solidly for a few days and if you're unlucky enough to live near a river you get a few feet of water surging through your house until the waters subside.
The flood that God sent was *completely* different.

For a start it was very, very sudden.

Let's be honest, if it *had* happened gradually then Noah's neighbors would have realized that he wasn't completely stark staring mad after all.

They'd probably have tried to cadge a ride just in case it got any worse.

So, a *slow* flood was out of the question.

But how could God flood the earth so quickly that people weren't able to escape?

Well, if God was going to use just rain, then that would *never* do the job.

Even if God emptied out every last drop of water that he'd been storing in the sky there wouldn't be anywhere near enough of it to cover the highest mountains.

Fascinating Fact:

The Bible tells us that as well as there being water in the sky and in the oceans, there is water stored under the earth.

Added together, this would have been plenty to cover the whole earth with water.

The Bible also says that the water rose to a level of over seven yards above the mountains. Deep or what?!

MAKE YOUR OWN FLOOD !!!

INSTRUCTIONS:-

1. Cut out the picture of the world

2. Place the world on a saucer or any other suitable waterproof container

3. Add water and there you have it... your very own flood!

HANDY TIP ~ FOR ADDED ENJOYMENT, FLOAT A MATCH AND PRETEND IT'S THE ARK!

HOURS OF FUN FOR ALL THE FAMILY

SAFETY WARNING: ALWAYS MAKE SURE THAT AN ADULT IS TO HAND WHEN COVERING THE WORLD WITH A CATASTROPHIC FLOOD!!!

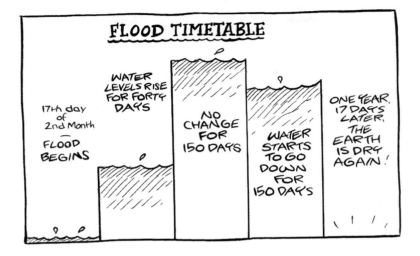

Ark Joke

Why didn't the ark have a horn?
Because with all those animals on board it **HONKED** enough already.

I wonder what Noah and his family were thinking as they looked out from the safety of the ark at the world around them disappearing before their very eyes.

They must have felt very sad.

Perhaps they even felt a bit lonely as they bobbed up and down on the rising flood.

Imagine being the last eight people left in all the world.

When the waters receded there wouldn't be anyone else except them.

No friends to visit.

Nobody else to talk to.

It must have felt quite strange.

Are We There Yet?

I'll bet that's what *you* say when you're on a long journey.

We asked our artist to think of some ways *Noah's* sons, Shem, Ham and Japheth might have passed their time on the ark.

Pull The Plug

There's two good ways of getting rid of water.

Getting it to drain away somewhere or drying it up.

When God needed to remove the flood waters from the face of the earth he used both methods.

The waters that had erupted out from under the earth were allowed to drain back.

And the remainder of the water God dried up with a powerful wind.

On the seventeenth day of the seventh month the ark came to rest on the mountains of Ararat.

Being a wise man, Noah decided not to let the animals out quite yet.

He waited another 40 days and then sent out a raven to check things out. The raven decided to make the most of his new-found freedom by clearing off for good.

So, God sent out a dove instead. The dove didn't have any luck finding a place to land but at least he returned to Noah.

A week later, Noah had another go with the dove and this time it came back by nightfall with a fresh olive leaf in its beak. Probably the first game of 'Fetch' in the history of the world. (Dogs were only used later when it wasn't quite so wet!!!)

This was the proof Noah was waiting for.
The water was well and truly going down.
Fasten your seatbelts, we're coming in to land.

Seven days later, Noah sent the dove out on its last mission.
It never returned.
At last it had found a place to settle.

One year and seventeen days after Noah, his family and all the animals had entered the ark the door was once again opened and out they all came.

As the animals went *into* the ark in groups of their kind, so they went *out* again.

Can you remember Abel, way back at the beginning?
He offered a sacrifice of thanks to God.
Being a good man, that's the first thing Noah did when he'd left the ark.
Noah built an altar which is really just a rock platform and then took one of every kind of ritually clean bird and animal and burned them on the altar.
The Bible says that God was pleased with Noah's offering.

Long Range Weather Forecast

God promised that he would never ever send another world-destroying flood.

The Sort Of Food People Used To Eat Before The Flood

TODAY'S MENU

GREEN PLANT SOUP
GREEN PLANT RISOTTO
GREEN PLANT and CHIPS
GREEN PLANT SURPRISE
(guess what the surprise
is? Yep, it's green plants!)
GREEN PLANTS and
CUSTARD

The Sort Of Food People Used To Eat After The Flood

TODAY's MENU

CHICKEN CURRY
PRAWN COCKTAIL
STEAK and CHIPS
BEEF SURPRISE
(guess what the
surprise is? No green
plants!!!)
SAUSAGES and
CUSTARD

Up until now, *everyone* was vegetarian.

After the flood, for whatever reason, God allowed people to eat meat.

Which is good news for people who sell hamburgers.

A lettuce leaf in a bun isn't quite the same, is it?

(Some Final Instructions From God)

DON'T EAT MEAT WITH BLOOD STILL IN IT!
(BECAUSE THE LIFE IS IN THE BLOOD.)

IF ANYONE KILLS ANOTHER PERSON
THEY MUST LOSE THEIR LIFE!
(BECAUSE PEOPLE ARE MADE IN
GOD'S LIKENESS.)

HAVE HEAPS OF CHILDREN!
(BECAUSE YOU'VE GOT TO
REPOPULATE THE EARTH.)

God's Promise

Have you ever seen a courtroom scene on TV where the witnesses place their hands on the Bible and promise to tell the truth.

The Bible is a reminder that God is *also* watching and if they lie then God will know even if nobody else does.

Just before Noah and his family went out to start their new lives, God made a promise with them which we've already mentioned.

God promised that never again would God destroy the earth with a flood.

As a sort of reminder, God would put a rainbow in the sky.

You might not think that a rainbow is a very original idea.

But that's *exactly* what it was...an ORIGINAL idea.

There'd never been a rainbow before because there'd never been rain.

As the clouds drifted away and the sun came out the world's first rainbow formed in the sky to prove to Noah that what God was saying was true.

The good thing was that the promise still holds for you and me.

It's like God's handshake on the deal.

Fascinating Fact:

There are stories about the Flood and Noah in the traditions of most cultures and civilizations including those of Britain, the Native Americans, Greece, Egypt and India.

Back To Work

After up to 100 years building a boat and then another year at sea, Noah must have been itching to get back to his old job of farmer.

So, it comes as no surprise that the Bible says that Noah planted a vineyard after he'd left the ark.

Not only was Noah possibly the first man to make wine but he might have also been the first man to get drunk.

Which is what the Bible unfortunately says happened to him.

How Do We Know That Noah Was A Real Person?

If the Bible is to be believed, then it should be possible to trace every person and nation back to Noah.

The Bible tells us that Noah's three sons, Shem, Ham and Japheth, went out into all the world to repopulate it.

It even gives us some pretty detailed family trees of their descendants and where they settled.

If that's true then ancient records from around the world should *also* say much the same thing.

Amazingly they do!

A lot of people think Noah and the ark is just a myth and a made up story.

That couldn't be further from the truth.

Okay, put your funny hats on and let's do what the archaeologists do...go digging!

To find what we're looking for we're going to need to track down some really ancient documents...

I'm afraid that they're going to need to be a lot, lot older than even *that*.

What we're looking for are ancient writings that go back thousands of years, like these...

Here's some of the info we've discovered from these and other ancient records.

Shem, Noah's eldest son, had five boys of his own.

There was Elam, Asshur, Aram, Lux and Arphaxad.

Elam was the founder of the Elamites who were known to the Babylonians as the Elamatu.

Asshur gave his name to Assyria whose first king was none other than Puzur Asshur I.

Aram was the founder of the Arameans.

We'll leave Lud and Arphaxad for now.

Fascinating Fact:

Abram, a famous guy from the next Holy Happenings book -
'Hodgepodge Hebrews', was Shem's great, great, great,
great, great, great, great grandson!

Ham, Noah's second son, had four sons, Cush, Mizraim, Put and
Canaan.
Canaan is in fact the name of the land the Israelites settled in.
Cush also had a place named after him near Egypt.
Tradition has it that many of us can trace our ancestry to Noah.
Japheth, Noah's third son, had seven boys.
Japheth is recorded in history as the founder of all the
Indo-European peoples.
The Irish can even trace themselves straight back to Japheth.
So can the Saxons who altered his name to Sceaf.
In India he was known as Pra-Japti and in Greece as Jupiter.

Just as staggering is that ancient records from early Britain show
that the Romans, Britons, Saxons and Goths all are direct
descendants of Noah.

No More Noah

At last it's time to say farewell to our friend, Noah.
950 years is a long time to have known him but even *he* can't live forever.

Just imagine the party he'd have had if he'd lived to 1,000.
It would have cost Shem, Ham and Japheth a small fortune.
As it was, he didn't quite make it.

Living another 350 years after the Flood still isn't bad going in anyone's book.

Right, that's just about it for *this* Holy Happenings book but the death of Noah doesn't quite wrap things up. There are a few more things you need to know before we go our separate ways. The *good* news is that there are no more floods to worry about ...

The *bad* news is that Noah's descendants are about to slip back into those old bad ways that brought on the flood in the first place. Read on ...

The Wild, Wild...East?

If you've ever seen those films about the first pioneer settlers of the wild west of America then you've probably got a good idea what it was like for Noah's sons and their families as they moved out to settle in new lands.

It was tough going.

The Bible says that they wandered about until at last they came to a plain in Shinar...

No, not *that* kind of plane.
A *plain*.

A big open piece of ground.
In fact, it was sort of around here...

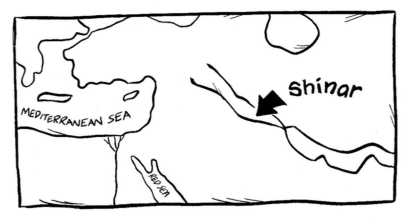

Tower Trouble!

It had to happen sooner or later.

God might have washed away all of the sinful people from the face of the earth but *sin* was still there, lurking *inside* of Noah's descendants.

The settlers in Shinar decided that together they could do almost anything.

They'd soon enough forgotten about the God that their dad, Noah, worshiped.

They were going to invent their *own* sort of gods.

Their gods wouldn't keep going on about sin.

They would be much more fun.

The settlers became so proud of how brilliant they thought they were that they decided that they weren't going to spread out right across the world like God had commanded them to do.

They were going to stay right where they were.

No one was going to push *them* around.

And to show who's boss, they built a city and a tower.

Now who were the clever ones?

Hang on a minute, did you say a tower?

What use is a tower?

Was it going to be like the Eiffel Tower to attract the tourists?

Seems a bit of a strange thing to build if you ask me.

A theme park or a shopping mall, maybe, but a tower, whoever heard of anything so silly?

PAY ATTENTION, CLASS! TODAY WE WILL BE LOOKING AT TOWERS, IN PARTICULAR, THE TOWER OF BABEL OR BABYLON (BECAUSE THAT WAS WHERE IT WAS BUILT, IN THE PLAIN OF SHINAR). THIS TOWER WAS MADE OF MUD, BRICKS AND HELD TOGETHER WITH TAR. LONG AGO, GODS WERE WORSHIPED ON MOUNTAINS OR HIGH PLACES. THE PLAIN OF SHINAR HAD NO MOUNTAINS BECAUSE IT WAS A PLAIN! WHICH IS WHY THEY BUILT THIS TOWER MADE OF STEPS OR AS IT WAS OFTEN CALLED, A 'ZIGGURAT', SO THAT THEY COULD GO UP TOWARDS HEAVEN, AS THEY BELIEVED, AND WORSHIP THEIR GODS. CLASS DISMISSED!

The funny thing was that God could see what they were doing all along so God went *down* to check up on them before they'd even had a chance to go *up*.

God realized very quickly that if they continued the way they were going the world was going to be as wicked as it had been before.

God couldn't send another flood.

God had already promised not to do *that* again.

I'll tell you what God did instead in a bit but first see if you can understand what these people are saying.

A bit tricky, huh?

Unless, that is, you happen to speak any of those languages.

Actually they're all saying the same thing - **"Thank You Very Much."**

If it hadn't been for that mud brick tower we'd all speak the same language.

God chose to mix up the language the first earth-dwellers used so they couldn't understand a word each other was saying.

That way they wouldn't be able to work together against God.

Holy Happenings Wild Guess: When God mixed up people's languages at Babel it must have sounded like a lot of BABBLE. I wonder if that's where it comes from?

With their language confused, God scattered the people to the four corners of the earth, to where God had originally instructed them to go.

And that's where our next Holy Happenings book begins when we start to take a look at those *Hodgepodge Hebrews* and their amazing adventures with God.

See you there!

The Bit at the End

Just before you leave, here's a reminder of some of the stuff we've been looking at.

First off....

What's Been Happening?

Before anything happens, God is already on the scene.

God creates the whole whopping great universe which includes the earth (obviously).

God makes the first people using unconventional methods. (One is made out of mud and the other out of a rib but they still turned out to be a nice looking couple.)

People turn against God in the Garden of Eden with a little help from a snake.

The first child is born.

The second child is born.

The first child murders the second child.

People go from bad to worse.

God tells Noah to build a big wooden box.

God destroys the wickedness of the world with a flood.

Noah, his family and oodles of animals are given a second chance.

Noah gets drunk.

People get a bit too big for their own boots and build the Tower of Babel.

God confuses their language and then scatters them across the earth.

A Reminder Of The Main Characters

God, (well, of course!).
Adam (the first man).
Eve (Mrs Adam).
The snake also known as the Devil, God's No.1 enemy.
Cain (Adam and Eve's first child).
Abel (their second son).
Noah (a good man).
A dove (Noah's look-out bird).
Methuselah (the world's oldest man).
Shem, Ham and Japheth (Noah's kids).

Your Turn

Write down what bits of the Bible you *don't* find boring any
more...

Why not get your hands on a real Bible and check out some of
the stuff we haven't had room to put in. There are loads of great
versions that don't use old-fashioned language and make it
really easy to read.
Happy reading!

HERE ARE SOME **BITESIZE** -BITS- OF THE BIBLE

(JUST TO GIVE YOU A TASTE OF A **REAL** BIBLE!)

GO ON—HAVE A NIBBLE!

In the beginning, when God created the universe, the earth was formless and desolate. The raging ocean that covered everything was engulfed in total darkness, and the power of God was moving over the water. Then God commanded, "Let there be light" - and light appeared. God was pleased with what he saw. Then he separated the light and the darkness, and he named the light "Day" and the darkness "Night". Evening passed and morning came - that was the first day.

Genesis 1: 1 - 5

CHEW!

NIBBLE!

Then God said, "And now we will make human beings; they will be like us and resemble us. They will have power over the fish, the birds, and all animals, domestic and wild, large and small." So God created human beings, making them to be just like himself. He created them male and female, blessed them, and said, "Have many children, so that your descendants will live all over the earth and bring it under their control."

Genesis 1: 26 - 28

And so the whole universe was completed. By the seventh day God finished what he had been doing and stopped working. He blessed the seventh day and set it apart as a special day, because by that day he had completed his creation and stopped working. And that is how the universe was created.

Genesis 2: 1 - 4

MUNCH!

CHEW!

CHOMP!

Now the snake was the most cunning animal that the Lord God had made. The snake asked the woman, "Did God really tell you not to eat from any tree in the garden?"

"We may eat the fruit of any tree in the garden," the woman answered, "except the tree in the middle of it. God told us not to eat the fruit of that tree or even touch it; if we do, we will die."

The snake replied, "That's not true; you will not die. God said that, because he knows that when you eat it you will be like God and know what is good and what is bad."

The woman saw how beautiful the tree was and how good its fruit would be to eat, and she thought how wonderful it would be to become wise. So she took some of the fruit and ate it. Then she also gave some to her husband, and he also ate it.

Genesis 3: 1 - 6

Then the Lord God said, "Now the man has become like one of us and has knowledge of what is good and what is bad. He must not be allowed to eat fruit from the tree of life, and live forever."

So the Lord God sent him out of the Garden of Eden and made him cultivate the soil from which he had been formed.

Genesis 3: 22 - 23

Then Adam had intercourse with his wife, and she became pregnant. She bore a son and said, "By the Lord's help I have acquired a son." So she named him Cain. Later she gave birth to another son, Abel.

Then Cain said to his brother Abel, "Let's go out in the fields." When they were out in the fields, Cain turned on his brother and killed him.

Genesis 4: 1 - 2 and 8

CHEW!

MUNCH!

When the Lord saw how wicked everyone on earth was and how evil their thoughts were all the time, he was sorry he had ever made them and put them on the earth. He was so filled with regret that he said, "I will wipe out these people I have created, and also the animals and birds, because I am sorry that I made any of them." But the Lord was pleased with Noah.

Genesis 6: 5 - 8

CHEW!

NIBBLE!

SLURP!

The Lord said to Noah, "Go into the boat with your whole family; I have found that you are the only one in all the world who does what is right. Take with you seven pairs of each kind of ritually clean animal, but only one pair of each kind of unclean animal. Take also seven pairs of each kind of bird. Do this so that every kind of animal and bird will be kept alive to reproduce again on the earth. Seven days from now I am going to send rain that will fall for forty days and nights, in order to destroy all the living beings I have made." And Noah did everything that the Lord commanded.

Genesis 7: 1 - 5

When Noah was 600 years old, on the seventeenth day of the second month all the outlets of the vast body of water beneath the earth burst open, and all the floodgates of the sky were opened and rain fell on the earth for forty days and nights.

Genesis 7: 11 - 12

MUNCH!

SLURP!

NIBBLE!

When Noah was 601 years old, on the first day of the first month, the water was gone. Noah removed the covering of the boat, looked round, and saw that the ground was dry. By the twenty-seventh day of the second month the earth was completely dry.

God said to Noah, "Go out of the boat with your wife, your sons, and their wives. Take all the birds and animals out with you, so that they may reproduce and spread over all the earth."

Genesis 8 : 13 - 17

CHEW!

CHOMP!

God blessed Noah and his sons and said, "Have many children, so that your descendants will live all over the earth."

Genesis 9: 1

God said to Noah and his sons, "I am now making my covenant with you and your descendants, and with all living beings – all birds and all animals – everything that came out of the boat with you. With these words I make my covenant with you: I promise that never again will all living beings be destroyed by a flood; never again will a flood destroy the earth. As a sign of this everlasting covenant which I am making with you and with all living beings, I am putting my bow in the clouds. It will be the sign of my covenant with the world. Whenever I cover the sky with clouds and the rainbow appears, I will remember my promise to you."

Genesis 9: 8 - 15

CHEW!

MUNCH!